ALASKA

GALLERY BOOKS
An Imprint of W. H. Smith Publishers Inc.
112 Madison Avenue
New York City 10016

This edition first published in U.S.
in 1990 by Gallery Books,
an imprint of W.H. Smith Publishers, Inc.
112 Madison Avenue, New York, New York 10016

ISBN 0-8317-8827-5

Printed and bound in Spain

For rights information about the photographs in
this book please contact:

The Image Bank
111 Fifth Avenue, New York, NY 10003

Producer: Solomon M. Skolnick
Author: Jennifer Grambs
Design Concept: Lesley Ehlers
Designer: Ann-Louise Lipman
Editor: Joan E. Ratajack
Production: Valerie Zars
Photo Researcher: Edward Douglas
Assistant Photo Researcher: Robert Hale
Editorial Assistant: Carol Raguso

Title page: *The aurora borealis, or
"Northern Lights," is especially
visible during Alaska's long winter.
The spectacular effect is caused by
electrically charged particles—which
smash into atoms—and molecules
that absorb light and glow with color.*

Stormy twilight envelops the Brooks Range which forms a natural barrier between Arctic and Interior Alaska and encompasses vast areas of parkland wilderness. Overleaf, page left: Home of the Inupiat Eskimos, Barrow, 330 miles above the Arctic Circle, is the northernmost U.S. town. Petroleum and oil exploration is ongoing nearby. Overleaf, page right: Amounts of oil estimated at 9.6 million barrels and about 26 trillion cubic feet of natural gas have established Prudhoe Bay as the largest oil field in North America.

-·- POW MAIN -·-
POINT BARROW, ALASKA
HOME OF THE NORTHERN
MOST TOTEM POLE IN
THE WORLD.

Alaska is America's magnificent last frontier where rugged wilderness and stark serenity complement and contradict one another. Masses of wildflowers, reborn in this frozen land each Arctic spring, remind an awestruck traveler of the delicate yet powerful balance of nature Alaska struggles to protect. Here is our country's final example that our environment is awe-inspiring. Alaska charms our sensibilities while romancing our spirit.

Those of us who dream of visiting the Great Land, ALAKSHAK, as the Aleuts named it, have much to anticipate, whether our journey is one of body or spirit. Here, a visitor can truly become an adventurer free to explore the glorious expanses of wilderness that remain largely unsettled.

The small native populations of Eskimo, Indian, and

Top to bottom: *Eight hundred miles long, the trans-Alaska pipeline winds its way southward from Prudhoe Bay to the port of Valdez. This hardy Alaskan husky, peering out from behind the traditional sled-dog carrier, is a loyal traveling companion. An Iditarod musher, competing in the famous 1,158-mile race, endures a lonely journey across Norton Sound.* Opposite: *Once considered the Far North's most valuable means of transportation, the dogsled and team have almost entirely been replaced by the snowmobile.*

Aleut people in the more remote regions still maintain a somewhat primitive lifestyle that reflects a heritage undaunted by modern America. Meanwhile, the largely youthful pioneers who have more recently ventured up from the "lower 48" bring to Alaska an enthusiasm and commitment that enrich this tempestuous alternative to contemporary life. Although snowmobiles and small airplanes have all but replaced the traditional dogsled, it is doubtful that man-made conveniences are a priority for the average Alaskan.

Exploration of our 49th and largest state is an experience that can't be duplicated elsewhere. A journey may wind along a coastline that is approximately 33,000 miles long and, at its westernmost point, takes us within two-and-one-half miles of the U.S.S.R. Its northern boundary is a mere 1,300 miles from the North Pole. A trek throughout Alaska would mean experiencing temperatures that range from surprisingly temperate to far below freezing.

Preceding page: *Salmon, shown here on drying racks, is the mainstay of the Alaskan husky diet.* This page, top to bottom: *The Nugget Inn is a fitting name for this hotel in Nome, where back in 1899, fortune hunters prospected three million dollars' worth of gold dust from the town's black, sandy beaches. This is a tribute to the craftsmanship of the Eskimos who live and create their tribal crafts in Nome. Ivory is still carved by Eskimos on the Seward Peninsula.*

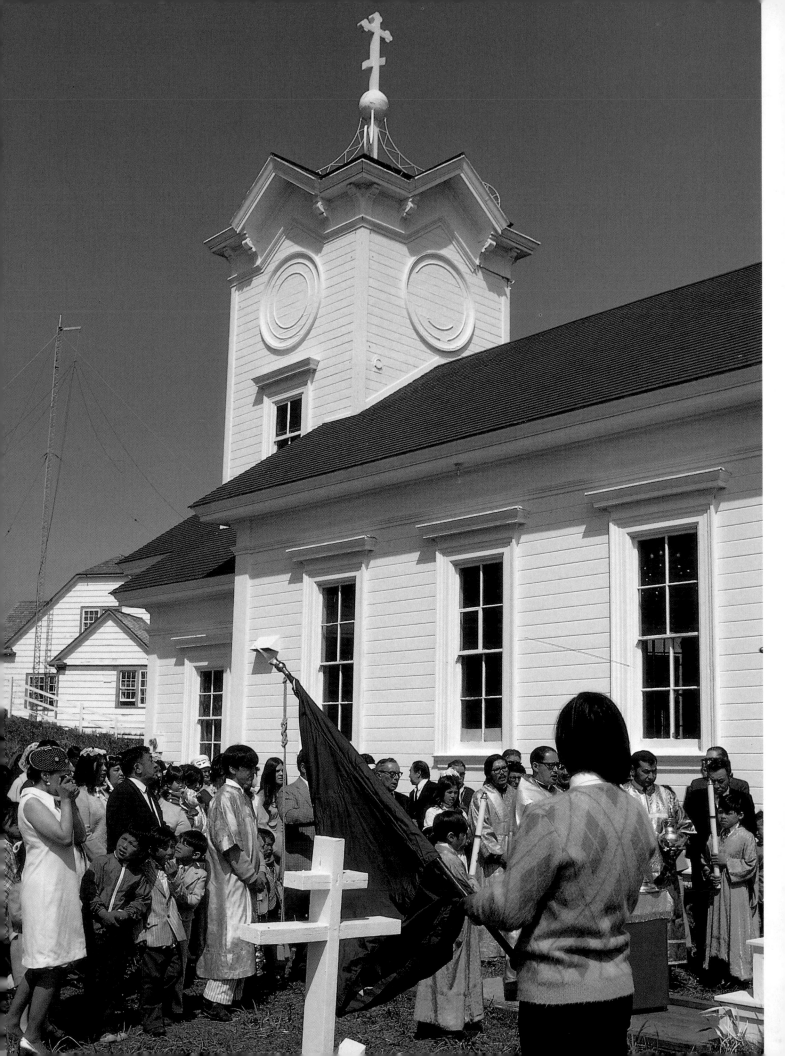

Preceding page: *A glimpse of one of St. Paul's Island's religious ceremonies.* This page: *This abandoned gold dredge is (top) in Fairbanks. The sternwheeler* Nenana *(bottom) is on display in Fairbanks' Alaskaland.*

Preceding page: *Gold dredges were engineering marvels, built to strip the earth in search of that precious metal. This one operated from 1930 to 1970.* This page, left to right: *The gorgeous stained-glass windows in Immaculate Conception Church contribute to its status as a National Historic Monument and to its popularity as a Fairbanks tourist-stop. A statue of Fairbanks' unknown first family, with the loyal husky at its side. A colorful fountain of flowers welcomes visitors to the University of Alaska campus at Fairbanks. Visitors can explore a gold-rush town at the 44-acre Alaskaland theme park.*

The trail would wind along millions of lakes, thousands of rivers, and then climb five mountain ranges, one of which boasts the highest peak in North America, the daunting 20,320-foot Mt. McKinley.

The enormous expanse of Alaska can be intimidating if we think in terms of the 586,400 square miles the state encompasses. A coastline, longer than that of the continental U.S., embraces several thousand glaciers, most of which date back at least 10,000 years to the Pleistocene Ice Age. Malaspina, a glacier the size of Rhode Island, is one of the largest.

Alaska's borders touch two oceans and three seas, and within these boundaries exotic and precious wildlife (largely undisturbed due to stringent conservationist laws) roam the countryside. Moose and caribou, black, brown, and grizzly bears share the environment with bison, wolves, foxes, and deer, to

Top to bottom: *The state-owned Alaska Railroad provides a scenic view of Denali National Park and Preserve when it traverses the 350-mile Fairbanks-to-Anchorage route through the park. The train depot at Denali merely hints at what lies ahead—9,375 square miles of primitive, unspoiled beauty. Visitors to Denali are on the lookout for the nearly 200 kinds of birds and wildlife that make the park their home.* Opposite: *Moose, brown bear, Dall sheep, and caribou casually go about their daily routines. Here, a moose grazes on the snow-laden vegetation of Denali.*

name a few. Polar bear and walrus are found in the most northern regions of Alaska. Board one of the many ocean liners and one is bound to spot otters, seals, whales, dolphins, and porpoises, while untold varieties of fish swim below.. A birdwatcher's paradise, Alaska boasts 397 species.

Alaska is also a botanist's dream. Masses of brilliantly colored flowers bloom during the spring and summer. Tiny wildflowers gloriously dot the tundra and alpine regions of the northern country, while larger varieties sprout in the meadows, forests, and valleys farther south.

The idea of wildflowers in Alaska may startle us, but no more so than the notion of somewhat balmy weather in a state usually associated with cold and ice. While temperatures can drop to minus 40-50 degrees in the Far North (where, even in July, only a few inches of ice melt), summer temperatures in the more southern areas can actually climb to the mid-80's.

As one proceeds north, the summer days get progressively longer and the winter days get progressively shorter. At the Arctic Circle, where an imaginary line 66°/33′ north of the equator crosses the upper third of Alaska, the sun doesn't set

The colors of the rainbow seem to be reflected in the peaks and valleys of this pass in Denali.

Toklat River tours are especially popular for photographers hoping to capture the beauty of the unusual tundra and abundant wildlife. Opposite: Mt. McKinley, whose 20,320-foot peak is the highest in North America, overlooks Wonder Lake in Denali Park.

Preceding page, top to bottom: *Nearly four miles high, Denali (The High One) is the Athabaskan Indian name for Mt. McKinley. A view of Polychrome Pass, where the thawed snow reveals the lush vegetation in the area.* This page: *Another Alaska Range peak in Denali glistens on a clear day.*

at all on midsummer days. During the winter solstice the sun never rises. This is the best time and place to see the aurora borealis, or Northern Lights, which illuminates the evening sky with brilliant color.

Alaska has endured a complicated and difficult history. Statehood was won in 1959, but only after two centuries of constant re-discovery. Russian sailors from Siberia first explored St. Lawrence Island in 1728. Thirteen years later, an expe-dition led by Vitus Bering reached the mainland. The lure of a land ripe for fur trading soon brought other Russian entrepreneurs who, more and more, invaded the Aleutian coast and set up fur trading posts. By 1784, the Russians had established the first permanent settlement on Kodiak Island.

Spanish and English exploration followed, but it wasn't until 1867 that the United States made a strong commitment to this uncul-tivated northern land. Secretary of State William Seward had the U.S. buy Alaska from Russia for $7.2 million, a move that was ridiculed by the public and the press as "Seward's Folly."

An image of Mt. McKinley mirrored in the lake below it. The mountain has two peaks and is covered by ice and snow most of the time.

But the unknown territory turned out to be a literal gold mine that cost the U.S. a mere two cents an acre.

The Gold Rush era between 1880 and 1902 unleashed a colorful episode of fortune hunters, boom towns, and about a billion dollars in gold. By 1912, Congress had accorded Alaska territorial status which led to its statehood a half-century later.

How to utilize Alaska's rich, natural resources while respecting the rights of its aboriginal people has always been a problem. But not until 1968, with the discovery of major oil deposits in the Prudhoe Bay area, did the very real issues of conservation and land rights present themselves. The Native Claims Settlement Act in 1971 helped to ease some tension. Yet, the trans-Alaska pipeline that daily pumps

Preceding pages, left: *The multi-colored sunset is reflected in one of the ponds nestled along the Alaska Range.* Preceding pages, right: *Cathedral Spires (top) in Denali National Park seem to burst from the clouds. The more earthbound Ruth Gorge (bottom).* Page left: *For the dozens of animals that roam the nearby park, Ruth Gorge, south of Denali, is not as inhospitable as it appears.* This page, top to bottom: *The Alaska Range includes Mt. Foraker, as well as lesser peaks. Caribous, set against a backdrop of mountains and sky, are at home on this range. Finding a wooden farmhouse in the Matanuska Valley may surprise an unsuspecting trekker.*

barrels of Alaska's "black gold" is a constant reminder of the need for guidelines. In an effort to conserve America's last great wilderness in 1980, President Carter signed the Alaska National Interest Lands Conservation Act that sets aside 104 million acres of new national parks, preserves, and recreation areas.

Perhaps the most spectacular way to approach Alaska from the "lower 48" is by a cruise ship that winds its way through the Inside Passage, part of the state-owned Alaska Marine Highways System. Since no roads connect the seaport towns that make up Alaska's panhandle, sea or air is the only way to experience the intricate network of inlets, fjords, coves, bays, and channels that line the passage. This unique route leads to mountains topped by giant glaciers that form massive ice

Preceding pages: *The aurora borealis lights up the dark northern sky in an ever-changing performance.* Page left: *Half of Alaska's population lives in modern Anchorage where a relatively moderate climate and its reputation as a major business and transportation center welcome new residents.* This page, top to bottom: *Hot-air balloon rides in Anchorage offer the more adventurous a view of the city's sophisticated skyline from a lofty perspective. The Anchorage Convention and Visitors Bureau is found on East Third Avenue. Anchorage's Iditarod Sled Dog Race begins each March and determines the world's best dog musher.*

Left to right: *Captain Cook Inlet is named for the British Captain James Cook, who discovered the site in 1778. Native spirit houses color and inspire the landscape at Eklutna. These signs point out that Anchorage is as far west as Hawaii and as far north as Helsinki.* Below: *This ice sculpture is part of the "Fur Rendezvous," a festival held each February.* Opposite: *The Cook Inlet oil capital of Kenai is the home of this old Russian Church which was established in 1894 and which contains century-old Russian art.*

fields up to 9,000 feet above the water. Lush valleys between the mountains seem carved into the earth.

Tucked between the mountains and the Pacific Ocean are about 1,000 islands. Some 54,000 people live on the nearly 600-mile-long panhandle, including native Tlingit, Haida, and Tsimshian Indians. Hand-carved totem poles are reminders of their rich Indian heritage and, at Ketchikan, the world's largest collection of totem poles is a tribute to this tradition. Ask someone who lives in Ketchikan, and the proud Alaskan will describe the state's southernmost city as "Five miles long, four blocks wide, and two blocks up Deer Mountain." He'll also comment on the city's claim as the world's salmon capital, but may not own up to the fact that, with a yearly rainfall of up to 162 inches, Ketchikan is the wettest place in the state.

Top to bottom: *A small boat harbor at Homer provides a tranquil view of the Chugach Mountains. In 1912, a great volcanic explosion transformed this once-peaceful valley into Katmai National Park and Preserve's Valley of Ten Thousand Smokes. Home of the kodiak brown bear (which can grow to nine feet), Kodiak is also known for its fishing, hunting, and wildlife watching.* Opposite: *Carved ages ago by glaciers that form the rugged coastline, the Kenai Fjords' waters are filled with porpoises, whales, seals, and sea otters.*

Alaska's Scandinavian heritage is probably most prevalent in Petersburg, famous for its shrimp industry, but remembered just as much by visitors for its colorful wooden homes, gaily decorated with floral artwork. Deservedly, Petersburg earns its nickname, "Little Norway."

Farther up the Inside Passage is Juneau, Alaska's capital and home of the famous Mendenhall Glacier, a 12-mile icy-blue river that melts into the massive Juneau Ice Field and is part of the Tongass National Forest. The old Russian capital of Sitka is a boat ride away.

Westward, around the Gulf of Alaska, this diversified land slips into the Kenai Peninsula (reappearing at its tip as Kodiak Island), where seals, whales, dolphins, other marine life, and many types of birds make their home in Kenai Fjord National Park. Its coastal area includes Prince William Sound and Valdez, the southern terminus of the trans-Alaska pipeline.

South Central Alaska reaches inland to the mighty Alaska Range, touching Denali National Park and Mt. McKinley. This area is home to about half of the state's population, 248,000 of whom live in Anchorage. Close to the

Roughly 580,000 acres of the Kenai Peninsula make up Kenai Fjords National Park. Its coastal mountain range includes the massive Harding Icefield, a reminder of the Ice Age.

Preceding page: *Seward is named for William H. Seward, who was responsible for the purchase of Alaska by the United States. The 1964 Good Friday Earthquake nearly devastated this port, but commercial fishing and shipping have brought the city back to health.* This page: *Frost (top) forms a glistening overcoat for the plant life of Chugach National Forest in South Central Alaska. Rabbit Lake (bottom) is a tranquil respite from the bustling city of nearby Anchorage. It's part of Chugach State Park which borders the city on the east, north, and south.*

ocean and yet shielded by mountains, this lively city is protected from the Arctic cold and maintains a reasonably moderate temperature year-round. Once a tent city for gold miners and fur traders, Anchorage is now a financial capital.

Aside from being at the heart of the South Central area, Anchorage is famous as the starting point of the yearly, grueling 1,158-mile

Preceding page: *An unusual hanging glacier in South Central Alaska is pictured here.* This page: *A tour boat (top) wends its way along Portage Glacier. Icebergs (right), some as high as 60 feet, have splintered from the glacier and settled into the 656-foot-deep lake.*

Seventy thousand people were involved in the making of the
trans-Alaska pipeline. This monument in Valdez, the pipeline's
southern terminus, is a reminder of Alaska's constant struggle
between conservation and progress. *Opposite: The harbor of
Valdez was pristine before an Exxon tanker plowed into Prince
William Sound's Bligh Reef in 1989, causing the nation's worst
oil spill.*

Mt. Marcus Baker, Prince William Sound.

Alaska is one of only three areas in the world enriched with tidewater glaciers—those that terminate in the ocean. Columbia Glacier, near Valdez, spans several miles. Below: *The blue color of glaciers, like Columbia, is caused by air bubbles in the compressed ice which absorb everything except blue light.*

Iditarod Trail Sled Dog Race that culminates in Nome. Despite a considerable shortage of women in a land where some adventurous men advertise for wives, musher Susan Butcher has won the race for four consecutive years.

South Central is also an area rich in mineral deposits. The minerals and the long summer daylight hours in the Matanuska Valley create fertile farmlands that yield outrageously large vegetables.

Kenai Fjords National Park is another lure to the peninsula. About 580,000 acres, it is the land of the massive Harding Icefield and the home of more than 23 marine mammal species, including seals and whales.

Kodiak, on Kodiak Island just south of the Kenai Peninsula, is Alaska's oldest community which dates back to 1784 when the Russian zeal for sea otter fur established it. Today, its Russian heritage is still evident in its Orthodox churches. The Kodiak National Wildlife Refuge there offers protection to the kodiak brown bear and to the endangered American bald eagle.

Top to bottom: *A man-in-the-moon view of a mountain near the Alaska-British Columbia border. A lone eagle soars above this tranquil valley on the peninsula that includes the Coast Range. Nearby, one of nearly 3,000 bald eagles that gather in their preserve from October through January to feed on Chilkat River salmon.*

The Alaska Peninsula, Kodiak Island's western neighbor, separates the Bering Sea from the Pacific Ocean. The seacoast wilderness provides ample romping space for the large population of brown bears in protected areas like Katmai National Park, much of which was created by the 1912 eruption of the now-dormant Novarupta Volcano. The mysterious Valley of Ten Thousand Smokes is also found here.

Swarms of prospectors gathered on Skagway's Broadway enroute to the dangerous Klondike during the 1898 gold strike. Right: Gold Rush Grove, Skagway, is testament to the outlaws and get-rich-quick prospectors who lost their lives here.

Rock walls rise majestically to heights of 3,000 feet at Misty Fjords National Monument in the Tongass National Forest east of Ketchikan. **Opposite:** *Flying high above Glacier Bay National Park provides a commanding view of seemingly ageless glaciers solidly perched atop Fairweather Range mountain peaks.*

Just past the tip of the peninsula, the Aleutian Islands begin a 1,500-mile sweep toward Asia. Mostly barren land, the islands are primarily inhabited by the Aleut Indians and native Eskimos. The area, including the Pribilof Islands, is a breeding ground of fur seal

Chartering boats for fishing or sightseeing is a popular adventure for visitors to Alaska's capital city, Juneau. Below: On board a cruise ship, one can glimpse the site of the gold rush of 1880 that brought hordes of gold-diggers northward. Opposite: Mendenhall Glacier, within walking distance of Juneau, provides visitors many gorgeous views.

CATHEDRAL PARK
JUNEAU
PARKS AND RECREATION

and sea otter, whose once certain extinction is being curtailed through conservation laws.

Interior Alaska and the Far North is a fantastic land filled with everything the average American has ever associated with Alaska: dog mushers, polar bears, ghost mining towns, Eskimos and Indians, and maybe the occasional igloo left behind by a tired hunter.

The Interior, sandwiched between the Alaska and Brooks Ranges, is the land of the Yukon River which courses across this 1,000 mile expanse from British Columbia to the Bering Sea. If interior Alaska is the heart of the state, the Yukon River is the pulse that gives it vitality.

Much of the region is wilderness, a large portion of which is comprised of national parks, preserves, and wildlife refuges. Practically smack in the middle of Alaska is the state's second largest city, Fairbanks. Once a gold rush town, it now houses Army and

Preceding page: *This Orthodox church is one of southeastern Alaska's oldest; its onion-domed architecture is a reminder of the state's Russian heritage.* This page, top to bottom: *An excursion along Juneau's Egan Drive is a chance to visit the capital's Centennial Hall Convention Center and its historical exhibits. Here, a celebration of Alaska's hard-won statehood. The governor's stately mansion graces Juneau.*

Air Force bases and the University of Alaska's main campus. It is also the northern gateway to Denali National Park and Mt. McKinley.

Above the Arctic Circle in the true Land of the Midnight Sun, the North Slope, permanently frozen in all its

Preceding page: *This totem pole, hand-carved from tall cedar logs, reflects the heritage of the large Tlingit, Haida, and Tsimshian Indian populations of the Ketchikan community.* This page: *Totem poles (top) are not used for worship: they either depict family lineage or simply tell stories. Totem Bight State Park (bottom), remarkable for its extraordinary collection of totem poles, is situated in a rain forest.*

Preceding page: *A view of Ketchikan's fishing vessel harbor (top) testifies to the soggy fact that this city is surely the wettest place in America—up to 162 inches of rain falls here each year. A historic district (bottom) has been established in Ketchikan which includes many houses built on stilts.* This page: *The Tlingit village of Angoon is Admiralty Island's only community. The Indians share their magnificent environment with vast brown bear and nesting bald eagle populations.*

600-mile-long glory, strains northward to reach the Arctic Ocean.

Eskimos and Athabascan Indians share this permanently frozen wilderness with grizzly bears, caribou, wolves, and foxes. Polar bears and seals live in the icy Arctic Ocean. Eskimo settlements of Nome, Kotzebue, and Barrow dot the landscape. Barrow, the northernmost settlement in North America and home to the Inupiat Eskimo, is where the Northern Lights shine most brightly and the temperatures drop to their lowest.

At Barrow, where the sun doesn't set from early May to August, wildflowers actually peek through the slightly thawed marshes until the winter months of perpetual darkness deny them light. Hard to imagine—in this seeming wasteland—that only 200 miles east at Prudhoe Bay, the continent's largest oil field pumps its precious liquid along its 800-mile journey to Valdez.

Alaska lives up to its nickname "The Last Frontier" and to its motto "North to the Future." Most of all, this fresh yet fragile land reflects the name of its state flower that urges us to "Forget-Me-Not."

Humpback whales, once numerous in coastal waters, are known for the arching formation of their leaps and dives.

Index of Photography